new dinos

THE LATEST FINDS! THE COOLEST DINOSAUR DISCOVERIES!

Written by Shelley Tanaka, Illustrated by Alan Barnard

Paleontological consultation by Dr. Philip J. Currie

AN ATHENEUM BOOK FOR YOUNG READERS / MADISON PRESS BOOK

New Dinosaurs

It seems unbelievable, but scientists estimate that only one percent of all the dinosaur species that ever lived have been found. This means that all the dinosaurs we know about — from *Tyrannosaurus rex* to *Velociraptor* — represent only a small sampling of the amazing creatures that lived on this planet for at least 165 million years.

About every seven weeks someone discovers the bones of a dinosaur no one has ever seen before. Sometimes the new finds reveal that our early ideas about dinosaurs were wrong. Other discoveries have shown that dinosaurs were not so different from creatures today.

Advanced technology allows us to learn more than ever from dinosaur fossils. High-powered electron microscopes reveal fine details of dinosaur feathers. A sophisticated X ray called a CT scan finds a heart inside a rib cage. Some scientists are trying to extract DNA from ancient eggs. Others are even studying fossilized dino dung to find out what dinosaurs ate.

Each new discovery and study provides clues to why these incredible creatures thrived for so long. How did they hunt? Raise their young? What sounds did they make? Are there even bigger, fiercer dinosaurs yet to be found?

Every day scientists find new answers to these questions, and many others. . . .

New Dinos of the Sahara

One hundred million years ago, in what is now known as Africa, the Sahara Desert was a lush forest laced with rivers where many creatures came to drink and to hunt. In 1997 paleontologists working in Niger found a dinosaur called *Suchomimus* ("crocodile mimic"), a deadly new species that looked like a *Tyrannosaurus rex* with the face of a crocodile. *Suchomimus* had big hands, with 9-inch (23-cm) thumbs topped by claws that were 7 inches (18 cm) long. Like giant gaffing hooks, these claws could spear a fish the size of a grown man. Once *Suchomimus* had shoveled the prey into its mouth, its one hundred hooked teeth would clamp down like huge pinking shears.

In 1995 paleontologists working in Morocco also found the bones of *Carcharodontosaurus*, an enormous carnivore. *Carcharodontosaurus* probably chased the large herbivorous dinosaurs, known as "sauropods," by running on its hind limbs and then slicing into the plant eaters with its bladelike teeth.

New dinosaurs are popping up all over the Sahara, an area so hot and remote that paleontologists have only begun to explore it in

Carcharodontosaurus

Suchomimus

Jobaria

the past ten years. In 1997 two new species of sauropod were found in Niger. *Jobaria*, the largest, was 66 feet (20 m) long and stood about 12 feet (3.6 m) at the shoulder. *Jobaria* had spoon-shaped teeth suited for nipping off the small branches of trees.

Nigersaurus was one of the smallest sauropods ever discovered — only 49 feet (15 m) long. So far not enough of its skeleton has been discovered to produce an accurate portrait. But we do know its large mouth contained about 600 teeth (though only about 110 of them showed when it smiled!). Beneath each tooth were up to seven replacement teeth, waiting like a stack of Dixie cups. New teeth were constantly growing from below, pushing out the old teeth as they wore down.

5

Deadlier than Dinosaurs SuperCroc!

Suchomimus and *Carcharodontosaurus* may have been deadly on land, but below the water lurked even bigger killers. For these ancient aquatic reptiles, a good-size dinosaur made a tasty meal.

On an expedition to Niger in 2000, researchers uncovered an ancient crocodile. *Sarcosuchus imperator* ("flesh crocodile emperor") was first discovered in the 1960s, but the new skeleton is the most complete, and one of the biggest, ever found.

Nicknamed "SuperCroc," *Sarcosuchus* lived 110 million years ago. It was as long as a school bus and weighed as much as a small whale. Its skull alone was as long as a grown man and contained a row of huge teeth, perfect for locking onto flesh.

With this kind of dental cutlery, *Sarcosuchus* likely ate more than just fish.

At the tip of SuperCroc's snout was a bony protrusion shaped like a toilet bowl. Scientists aren't sure what it was used for, but it may have heightened the croc's sense of smell or helped it to make loud mating calls. *Sarcosuchus* spent most of its time lurking underwater, its big eyes just breaking the surface, watching and waiting. When an unwary sauropod *(at right)* came to the river's edge and bent down to drink, *Sarcosuchus* would lunge out of the water and grab the dinosaur by the neck or leg.

What About T.rex?

T. rex's brain was smaller than
a head of broccoli — bigger than the brain of
any modern reptile, but much smaller than that of an
elephant or rhinoceros.

We know it was enormous and deadly, with a massive jaw full of teeth that could rip apart flesh and crush bones. In movies we've watched it running like the wind and ignoring prey that was right under its nose. But new discoveries are constantly changing our picture of this fearsome predator. In 1990 Sue Hendrickson found three large vertebrae poking out of a cliff in South Dakota. This was the first sight of the fossil named Sue — the most complete *Tyrannosaurus rex* ever found.

The prize piece of the fossil was its skull. The skull is the most useful part for paleontologists, since it reveals so much about an animal's feeding habits, senses, and intelligence. CT scans showed huge nasal passages and olfactory bulbs the size of grapefruits — almost as big as the rest of the brain. This means *T. rex* would have been extremely good at sniffing out prey with its powerful sense of smell.

In 1997 the skeleton of **Tyrannosaurus Sue** was bought by the **Field Museum in Chicago** for **$8.4 million (U.S.),** the most money ever paid for a fossil.

Bite Me!

T. rex had jaws adapted to bite deep and hard, even crunching through the neck or backbones of its prey. Studies have shown that *T. rex* had the most powerful bite force of any known animal — 3,000 pounds per square inch (200 kg/cm²) — enough to crush a pickup truck! A modern crocodile has just above 2,000 pounds (133 kg) of bite force, the highest ever measured in a living animal.

1 A walking *T. rex* steps forward with its tail held straight out behind for balance.

2 Shifting to the other foot, the dino's huge leg muscles help to support its massive weight.

Early studies of Sue's skeleton suggested that *T. rex* moved more quickly and elegantly than was previously thought. Sue's thigh bones extended straight down from the pelvis, which means the dinosaur didn't waddle but had a long, swinging stride like a human. It moved with its tail out, balanced to the rear.

Researchers had calculated that Sue probably covered 12 to 14 feet (3.6 to 4.2 m) with each step. But a 2002 study based on computer models claimed that the dinosaur's

The backward curve of Sue's enormous teeth kept food from slipping out of the dino's mouth.

Prehistoric Cannibals

Tyrannosaurus Steven, discovered in 1995, has bones missing from its loin section, and some vertebrae have been bitten in half. We know tyrannosaurs fought with each other (a jawbone found in Alberta has the broken tip of another tyrannosaur's tooth buried in the bottom of it). But they may also have eaten one another from time to time.

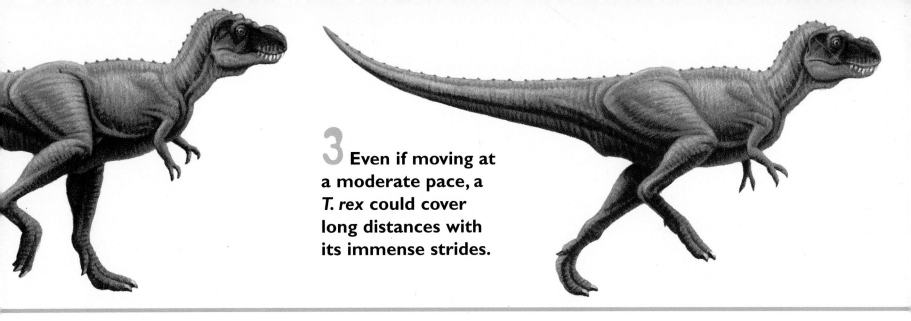

3 Even if moving at a moderate pace, a *T. rex* could cover long distances with its immense strides.

leg muscles were too small to allow it to run quickly, and that *T. rex* was probably no faster than a human. On the other hand, its prey was even slower!

T. rex was king of the dinosaurs, but that doesn't mean it was invulnerable. Sue was old and a bit of a wreck. There appears to have been an infection that left big holes in its lower jaw. Sue had also been bitten or cut on the lower leg bone — an infection that likely

oozed pus from time to time while it healed. The dinosaur suffered from gout (a joint disease that plagues many species, including birds, alligators, and humans), which would have caused throbbing joints, pain, and ill temper! There were broken and infected ribs, and several bones in the tail had stiffened and begun to fuse.

It seems life was tough sixty-seven million years ago, even for the biggest and the strongest.

Where Did T. rex Come From?

Tyrannosaurus rex fossils have only been found in western North America, but that doesn't prove they originated there. In 2001 scientists in England reported the discovery of *Eotyrannus*, a primitive tyrannosaur that lived long before *T. rex*.

Just because one dinosaur looks like another doesn't necessarily mean they are related. *T. rex*, for example, was descended from small meat eaters like *Velociraptor*, and is not related to look-alikes such as *Allosaurus*.

Who's the Biggest Carnivore?

Giganotosaurus's daggerlike teeth suggest it hunted dinosaurs many times bigger than itself. It could probably have taken down a plant eater as large as *Argentinosaurus*, the biggest dinosaur of any type ever found (plant-eating dinosaurs were often bigger than meat eaters). As one paleontologist said, "This was an animal that would run in, take a very large bite, then back off and watch. Basically the prey would bleed to death."

For the past few years this contest has been more or less a draw between *Tyrannosaurus rex* and *Giganotosaurus*, depending on who's doing the measuring and how the skeletons are reassembled. There is no doubt that *Giganotosaurus* had the longest skull, but *T. rex* was much taller at the hips, and the bodies of the two animals are about the same length. One thing is certain — they were all bigger than a double-decker bus!

Over the past few years, scientists in Patagonia have been digging up the bones of what could be the biggest meat-eating dinosaur on record. Closely related to *Giganotosaurus*, the unnamed creature is estimated to be 46 feet (14 m) long — perhaps the biggest carnivore yet. It is thought to be bigger than the 45-foot (13.5-m) long Celeste, discovered in 2000 in Eastern Montana and the largest *T. rex* found to date.

Tyrannosaurus (Sue)

Found: South Dakota,
       1990 (90 percent recovered)
Lived: 67 million years ago
Length: 39 feet (11.8 m)
Height at hip: 11 feet (3.4 m)
Weight: 7 tons (6.3 T)
Length of skull: 5 feet (1.5 m)
Teeth: thick and strong, good for crushing bones

Giganotosaurus

Found: Patagonia,
       1993 (80 percent recovered)
Lived: 100 million years ago
Length: 40 feet (12.2 m)
Height at hip: 10 feet (3.1 m)
Weight: 8 tons (7.1 T)
Length of skull: 6 feet (1.8 m)
Teeth: blade-shaped and serrated, good for ripping
       flesh and bloodletting

Hunting for Dinner

Meat-eating dinosaurs probably adopted one of three hunting techniques used by carnivores today. Some, like *Utahraptor*, might stalk prey (like a cat after a mouse), step by step: **(1)** with its long tail stretched out behind for balance, **(2)** at the right moment the raptor would pounce forward, **(3)** grabbing and kicking the prey with its hind limbs and disemboweling it with its enormous claws.

Other dinosaurs, like *Suchomimus*, might suddenly lunge for prey like a crocodile, biting down quickly on the neck or back.

Dinosaurs like *Velociraptor* may have chased down prey, like a cougar after a deer, jumping up again and again to weaken the quarry before the final kill.

(Opposite) *Amid a cloud of dust stirred up during the attack, a pack of tyrannosaurs is able to bring down a lone Hypacrosaurus, a huge duck-billed herbivore.*

Hunting in Packs

For a long time experts assumed that large meat-eating dinosaurs lived and hunted alone. But on annual expeditions to Patagonia from 1997 to 2000, researchers found the remains of a new unnamed species closely related to *Giganotosaurus*. Seven individuals of different ages were buried in one spot, so the large carnivores may in fact have moved in packs, teaming up to take down giant sauropods like *Argentinosaurus*.

At about the same time, the remains of several *Albertosaurus* dinosaurs (relatives of *T. rex*) were found in a seventy-million-year old riverbed in western Canada. The bones of a dozen individuals, including teenagers, parents, and a six-month-old baby, were found together. Ancient charcoal found near the site suggests the pack might have been running to the river to escape a forest fire.

Monsters of Madagascar

The red soils of Madagascar, an island located off the east coast of Africa, have given up some of the most important dinosaur remains found in the past few years.

In 1998 paleontologists announced the discovery of two new carnivores. *Majungatholus* (*below, top left*) had wicked serrated teeth and a fat, bull-like head with a thick dome above its eyes. It probably preyed on huge, long-necked sauropods. *Majungatholus* was closely related to *Carnotaurus*, a dinosaur found on the other side of the planet in South America.

The discovery of a new buck-toothed dinosaur called *Masiakasaurus knopfleri*, named after Dire Straits' lead singer, Mark Knopfler, was announced in 2001.

Workers listened to the band's music while digging, and thought it brought them luck. The size of a large dog, *Masiakasaurus (right)* appeared to need an orthodontist. Its long, cone-shaped teeth had hooked tips, and the lower front teeth stuck straight out — strange to look at, but ideal for spearing the fish, snakes, and small mammals that made up this creature's diet.

The Oldest Dinosaur?

Until recently *Eoraptor* (discovered in 1991) was considered to be the oldest dinosaur ever found. The dog-size meat eater from Argentina lived 228 million years ago. But in 1999 scientists announced the discovery of an as-yet-unnamed new prosauropod (an early plant eater) in Madagascar. About the size of a kangaroo, it lived 230 million years ago, which would make its fossils the oldest dinosaur bones ever found.

Shifting Continents

About 210 million years ago, all the land on Earth was lumped into a single mass called Pangaea ("whole earth"). Then, 170 million years ago, Pangaea began to break into two main chunks — Gondwana in the south and Laurasia in the north. Eventually Gondwana broke up to form Africa, Antarctica, South America, Australia, India, and Madagascar. Laurasia became North America, Greenland, Northern Europe, Asia, and Siberia.

Finding dinosaurs as similar as *Majungatholus* and *Carnotaurus* so far apart means Madagascar and South America were joined together longer than scientists once thought, or were perhaps connected by Antarctica. New dinosaur discoveries are helping geologists to determine how and when the continents formed.

210 MILLION YEARS AGO   **TODAY**

Triassic Period
(248 – 213 million years ago)

Jurassic Period
(213 – 144 million years ago)

Cretaceous Period
(144 – 65 million years ago)

An Inside Look

Paleontologists usually find the remains of hard tissue such as bones, teeth, and claws. Soft tissue such as the internal organs, skin, and flesh generally decompose before they can turn into fossils. We know that dinosaurs had intestines, lungs, hearts, and brains, but we do not often see the real thing.

In 1995 an amateur fossil hunter in Italy saw the movie *Jurassic Park* and noticed the resemblance between *Velociraptor* and a small fossil that he had in his collection. He took his fossil to a museum, where paleontologists said it was indeed a baby dinosaur — a new theropod that lived 113 million years ago. They called it *Scipionyx*. It was the first dinosaur ever to be found in Italy.

Scipionyx had been buried in fine sand at the bottom of a shallow lagoon. Because it had been preserved in an almost oxygen-free environment, scientists hoped the specimen had fossilized before all the flesh had decomposed. When they studied the skeleton, they found even more than they had hoped for, including the dinosaur's windpipe, colon, and what appears to be muscle tissue.

How Do We Know Scipionyx Was a Baby?

Scipionyx (model shown top right) **was probably only a few weeks old. From its fossil *(below right)* we know the ends of its bones had not yet hardened and its eyes and head were large in proportion to its body. As an adult it would have been about the size of a Labrador retriever.**

Dinosaur with a Heart

In 1993 diggers in South Dakota found the remains of a pony-size plant eater called *Thescelosaurus* (nicknamed "Willo"). Willo lived sixty-six million years ago, but the dinosaur was amazingly well preserved. Bits of tendon and cartilage were still attached to the bones. When researchers noticed a reddish, grapefruit-size lump of rock behind the ribs, they wondered whether it might contain the dinosaur's internal organs.

It took several years of study to find the answer. Finally in 2000, scientists announced that CT scans had given them the first-ever look at a dinosaur's heart. Several cardiologists and veterinarians examined the scans and found that the heart had four chambers and a single

(Left) *Willo's heart is the round mass in the center of the photo.* (Above) *What Willo might have looked like.*

aorta. "It was an incredible sight," said one scientist, "because it turned out to be a ringer for the heart of a mammal or bird today."

If the dinosaur's heart resembled those of warm-blooded creatures instead of reptiles, could that mean its behavior did too? Some experts think a four-chambered heart means the dinosaur was warm-blooded and had a complicated circulatory system. Others think Willo was cold-blooded but had a high-performance heart that allowed it to move quickly for long periods.

Warm-Blooded vs. Cold-Blooded

For a long time paleontologists thought dinosaurs were *ectotherms* — slow-moving cold-blooded creatures like crocodiles and lizards. (Unable to control their body temperature, ectotherms must bask in the sun to warm up their blood enough for them to move quickly.) But as scientists considered how dinosaur bones were put together and how the animals moved, new theories developed.

Maybe meat-eating dinosaurs were warm-blooded *endotherms*, just like humans and birds. Endotherms can keep their blood warm no matter what the outside temperature. Active when they want to be, they can chase prey and travel long distances without taking a break. But large warm-blooded animals must develop ways to vent off excess heat. Humans perspire when they get hot. Elephants shed heat through the extra surface of their big ears. Large dinosaurs may have used their head crests, sails, and frills for cooling purposes.

Maybe some dinosaur species were warm-blooded and some were not. Or perhaps some were warm-blooded at birth but became ectotherms when they grew large enough to have problems getting rid of excess body heat.

The Feathered Dinos of Liaoning, China

This farmland in northeast China was built on ancient volcanoes. About 120 million years ago, the area was home to a rich variety of ancient plants and animals, including dinosaurs. From time to time the volcanoes erupted, covering the land and lakes with thick layers of fine ash. Plants, reptiles, fish, birds, insects, bacteria, small mammals, and dinosaurs were buried under a blanket of sediment, leaving fossils so detailed that even soft structures like feathers can be seen.

Most paleontologists now agree that some time before 145 million years ago, two-legged theropod dinosaurs similar to *Velociraptor* began to evolve into modern birds. Birds and theropods have many similar skull and skeleton characteristics that are not found together in any other group of animals. They also share behaviors such as sitting on nests and feeding their young.

The recent discovery of numerous feathered dinosaurs in Liaoning, China, provides a solid link between dinosaurs and birds. Many experts now think advanced theropods like *Velociraptor* had feathers, making them look more like weird birds than giant lizards.

In 1999 paleontologists found a turkey-sized dinosaur that was covered with downy feathers. *Sinornithosaurus (opposite)* couldn't fly, but unlike other birdlike dinosaurs (which had limited movement in their upper arms), it may have been able to move its long arms up and down similar to the way birds move their wings. It lived 125 million years ago and may have moved its arms to help it keep its balance while running. This dinosaur also had teeth like a barracuda's and long killer claws on its feet and hands.

In 2000 another dinosaur fossil was discovered that had feathers all over its body. Scientists are not sure whether the fossil is a new species or a juvenile *Sinornithosaurus*. It is further evidence that modern birds are the descendants of dinosaurs. This dinosaur is 130 million years old and looked like a duck with a reptile's tail. It had a wishbone and birdlike toes. The head and tail were covered with downy fluff. Though the arms were too short to support wings, they show the clear imprint of feathers resembling those on a modern bird.

Not Flying Dinosaurs

They looked like dinosaurs and they flew like birds. But they were neither. Flying reptiles called pterosaurs lived alongside the dinosaurs. Like the dinosaurs, they became extinct around sixty-five million years ago.

Tapejara Imperator

Crowded Skies

Birds lived at the same time as the pterosaurs and dinosaurs (the earliest known true bird, *Archaeopteryx*, lived 145 million years ago). All of them had feathers, but not all flew. Some were wiped out at the same time as the dinosaurs but others survived and evolved into modern birds.

How Did Dinosaurs Turn into Birds?

1 Short, downy feathers, once used for warmth, get bigger and stiffer on the arms and tail. The feathers develop into fans that can be used to attract mates and also give the animal an aerodynamic advantage.

2 The breastbone and wishbone (furcula) become anchors to support the powerful wing muscles needed for flight.

Bambiraptor

Pterosaurs looked more like bats than birds (some even had fur). Like *Tapejara imperator (left)*, they had thin, featherless wings made of skin. Their bones were eggshell-thin and hollow to make them light enough to fly. Though some were as tiny as sparrows, the largest was the size of a small airplane. They were the largest animals ever to fly.

3 The tail shrinks and the last five or six vertebrae fuse into a rod. In birds this rod supports the tail feathers used to stabilize flight.

4 Wings develop as wrist and fingers fuse into a shaft that can support the long, stiff feathers. Bones and joints in the shoulder and arm slowly change to produce the complex movements of flight.

Modern-day roadrunner

Raptors
From Mega to Micro

Megaraptor's *claw*
(above) *was about
five times bigger than
that of a large tiger. In
contrast* Microraptor's
*head (opposite) was
tiny. Both are shown
at life size.*

found. South America was also home to an ancient fish as long as a man, a 2-foot (60-cm) spider, and a crocodile the size of a school bus (see page 6). Scientists are still trying to figure out why the animals there grew so big.

In 2000 paleontologists in Liaoning, China, announced the discovery of the smallest dinosaur fossil ever found. The meat-eater *Microraptor* lived 125 million years ago and was about the size of a crow. It had feathers and may have lived in trees.

Did birds first learn to fly by leaping to the ground from high perches in trees, or did they run along the ground, flapping their arms until they took flight? The discovery of *Microraptor* may help to solve the mystery.

Most raptors were small enough to look a human child in the eye. But in 1999 paleontologists published new information on *Achillobator*, a new giant raptor found in Mongolia that was about 13 feet (4 m) long and probably weighed about 600 pounds (275 kg). And in 1997, scientists reported the discovery of what may be yet another huge raptor. *Megaraptor* had a 13-inch (33-cm) switchblade claw (*Velociraptor*'s claw was only half as long) and was big enough to take on large sauropods.

Megaraptor was unearthed in northwestern Patagonia, the same place where the enormous dinosaurs *Giganotosaurus* and *Argentinosaurus* were

Plant-eating Giants

The Patagonian desert in
Argentina is considered the
richest source of dinosaur fossils in the southern hemisphere. Some of the most impressive finds
include new species of giant plant eaters called sauropods, the biggest creatures ever to walk the earth.

Argentinosaurus

This sauropod was found in 1990. It was so big that it took seven years
to excavate a partial skeleton. *Argentinosaurus* was only 90 feet (28 m)
long but was massive and may have weighed as much as
100 tons (90.7 T), which would make it the heaviest
creature ever to walk on land.

Rio Negro Giant

This as-yet-unnamed giant was found in Patagonia in
2000. It may turn out to be as long as 160 feet (48 m) —
the length of half a city block. At first researchers thought
its thick neck vertebrae were leg bones, they were so big.
The new dinosaur would have been longer than
Argentinosaurus, but it weighed much less. It may even have
been as long as *Seismosauras*, which was found in New
Mexico and is estimated to be 150 feet (45 m) long — the
longest dinosaur yet.

Diplodocus

A North American Giant — Sauroposeidon

When it was found in Oklahoma in 1994, this sauropod's bones were mistaken for tree trunks, they were so huge. With its 40-foot (12-m) long neck, *Sauroposeidon* ("earthquake god lizard") would have been able to peer into the top windows of a six-story building.

Supersonic Tails

A 1997 study suggested that sauropods could snap their long tails like bullwhips — fast enough to break the sound barrier. The action would have made an impressively loud crack. But sauropods wouldn't have used these whips as weapons, since striking at such a speed would break the fragile bones at the end of the tail. Instead they may have made the noise to attract mates or scare off rivals or predators.

Making Tracks

Sauropods migrated in herds, traveling from one feeding ground to another. With their huge appetites and heavy footsteps, there probably wasn't much greenery left once they had passed through.

In 2001 researchers in northwest China reported the discovery of footprints belonging to giant plant-eating dinosaurs. A single footprint was as big as a bathtub!

Monster Appetites

Most people think of sauropods as huge beasts stretching up their necks to nibble on treetops. But scientists have always wondered how their hearts could produce enough pressure to pump blood so high without exploding the blood vessels.

A 1999 study reveals that in fact many sauropods did not lift their heads much higher than shoulder level. They stood with their necks straight out, heads pointing to the ground, their long tails stretched behind for balance. Like long-necked vacuum cleaners, they would sway from side to side, scooping up ferns and low shrubs.

Sauropods were nonstop eaters (they probably even had to eat through the night). They didn't waste time chewing but simply gobbled down massive amounts of vegetation that was ground up inside their long guts.

Today many birds (such as chickens) swallow grit to help grind food; sauropods swallowed whole rocks. Some of these stones (called gastroliths) were as small as peach pits; others were the size of grapefruits. The stones helped grind up plants so they could be more easily digested.

Dino Dung

The largest dinosaurs were giant eating machines. While carnivores feasted on small mammals, fish, reptiles, and one another, huge sauropods crunched constantly on ferns, brush, and leafy branches.

All this eating produced lots of droppings. Usually the dung was trampled into the ground, where it became fertilizer. But some dinosaur dung patties have been preserved as fossils called coprolites. A 24-foot (7-m) long *Maiasaura* might leave patties the size of flattened volleyballs. Other specimens look like footballs.

Fossilized *T. rex* dung found in western Canada was 18 inches (46 cm) long and about 4 inches (10 cm) in diameter. Embedded in it were many bone fragments, suggesting that *T. rex* gobbled its food and didn't waste time eating around the bones.

The Real Poop

The vegetation found in the coprolites shown below suggests they came from titanosaurs. Herbivore dung fossils contain chewed bark, seeds, stems, and leaves; carnivore dung fossils contain pieces of bone, teeth, and fish scales. Knowing who ate what helps researchers reconstruct a picture of what daily life was like in ancient times.

Gathering Eggs

Dinosaur eggs have been found at about two hundred sites around the world. Some are round like soccer balls; others look like loaves of bread. Some look just like birds' eggs.

Eggs are especially informative when they contain embryos — the fossilized skeletons of unhatched baby dinosaurs. These embryos can tell us which species an egg belongs to, but they are rare, since their delicate bones tend to decompose long before they are fossilized.

Even when embryos have been found, the tiny bones have usually collapsed into a jumbled heap. Recently, paleontologists in China made one of the rarest finds of all — the skeleton of an embryo still lying curled in its original position in the egg. The dinosaur is thought to be a therizinosaur, a sharp-clawed meat eater.

In 1997 hundreds of eggs were found in Argentina. Several contained the jumbled embryos of titanosaurs, a family of sauropods that includes species such as *Argentinosaurus*. The cat-sized hatchlings would have grown into adults that were 45 feet (14 m) long.

The titanosaurs lived eighty million years ago, long after many other giant sauropods had become extinct. Their eggs even contained fingernail-sized

(Above) The embryo of a therizinosaur, still curled up inside its egg. (Right) Once thought to be an egg thief, Oviraptor was actually a devoted parent who carefully guarded its eggs.

patches of fossilized skin and peg-shaped teeth as small as the tips of ballpoint pens. The nesting grounds may have been suddenly flooded, burying the about-to-hatch eggs in mud. The huge nesting area — 13 miles (21 km) long and 4 miles (6 km) wide — also provides evidence that the dinosaurs returned year after year, leaving layers of eggshells and unhatched eggs.

Scientists have known for years that some dinosaurs cared for their young. Species that were too heavy to sit on the eggs may have covered them with vegetation. Others buried their eggs to keep them from drying out.

In 1994 paleontologists in Montana found nests of eggs containing embryos of the carnivore *Troodon*.

One nest contained the remains of an adult that may have been keeping the eggs warm. The eggs required such a long brooding time that the job may have been shared by both parents. There is no evidence that the *Troodon* parents cared for the babies once they hatched. But both adult and young skeletons were found at the nesting site, so these dinosaurs may have stayed in family groups only for protection or communal hunting.

Getting Attention

Like most vertebrate animals, dinosaurs were capable of making sounds. Some had fat bulbous noses that could have been blown like a horn. *Parasaurolophus* had a huge tubelike crest that extended more than 3 feet (90 cm) from the top of its head. Inside the tube were air passages that connected the nostrils with the back of the throat.

In 1995 a particularly well-preserved *Parasaurolophus* crest was found in New Mexico. CT scans showed that the crest contained a complicated network of hollow tubes that could have been used to make a distinctive sound when the animal blew through its nose. The sounds were probably produced in the throat and amplified in the crest like a megaphone. Computer models have produced the noises the dinosaur might have made seventy-five million years ago. The sounds could have been quite varied and might have been used to attract a mate, to frighten off predators or rivals, to call to young, or as warning or distress cries. It's possible dinosaurs could even recognize the individual calls of family members. The extra surface area provided by the giant headcrest may also have helped *Parasaurolophus* keep cool.

The fossil of Parasaurolophus's head crest (above) *and two models* (below).

In Living Color

Dinosaur artists base their illustrations on fossilized bones and on their knowledge of animal anatomy. But when it comes to soft tissue like noses, ears, bellies, eyebrows, cheeks, and eyes, much of what they do is simply guesswork. Would a dinosaur have droopy wattles like a turkey's or fat cheeks like a rabbit's? Yellow eyes like an owl's or brown like a dog's? We'll probably never know.

Though scientists have found dinosaur skin, they do not know what color it was, because skin pigments disappear soon after a creature dies. The colors seen on the frills of *Pachyrinosaurus (above left)* and *Styracosaurus (above right)* are what the artist imagined. However, many experts suspect dinosaurs could see color, just as birds do. If so, some may have worn bright shades to attract mates; others may have had camouflage colors to hide from predators.

CT scans and computer models can show us how dinosaurs made sounds, and how they heard them. Scans of the inner-ear structure of *Nanotyrannus* reveal that this relative of *T. rex* could have picked up the low-frequency sounds of its prey. The outer-ear canals also pointed to the front to draw in any sound in stereo, allowing the dinosaur to pinpoint the distance and direction of prey.

Old Bones, New Tech

Dinosaur digs are still located in some of the toughest terrain on the planet, and extracting dinosaur bones remains slow, picky, back-breaking work. Working on the blistering sands of the Sahara or Patagonian desert is so taxing that crew members can lose 20 pounds (9 kg) each during a month-long dig.

But these days paleontologists don't always have to rough it. They dine on freeze-dried dinners. They listen to their Discmans while they work, and at the end of the day they key in their notes on laptop computers. They communicate with museums and families by satellite phones. Satellite images are even used to help pinpoint places where fossils might be found.

Once fossils are in the laboratory, modern technology provides a whole new range of tools, including high-powered microscopes, CT scans, ultraviolet light, and computer programs that allow scientists to learn how dinosaurs moved and ate.

In the past, the only way to look inside a fossil was to cut it up or take it apart. Now researchers can see inside dinosaur skulls and skeletons. CT scans move around an object, taking thousands of X rays. These pictures are assembled by computers to provide a 3-D cross section, allowing scientists to study the inside of a fossil without cutting it open.

Dino Clones?

To create a living copy of a dinosaur, scientists would need to retrieve most of its DNA, the fragile and complex molecule that forms the blueprint of any creature. A few researchers claim to have found segments of dino DNA, but most experts suspect this is the result of contamination by non-dino DNA. (Even a speck of dust can hold bits of skin or hair that can contaminate a sample.) Many scientists believe that DNA falls apart too quickly to survive for millions of years. But the research continues, and someday soon we will know whether it is possible to clone a dinosaur or not.

What Did Dinos Really Look Like?

As new information becomes available, artists change the way they portray dinosaurs. (1) Years ago almost all illustrations of *Velociraptor* showed the dino as a scaly reptile. (2) As the links between dinosaurs and birds became more well known, some artists added birdlike feathers. (3) After recently found fossils of similar species revealed more hairlike feathers, many artists have changed the portraits yet again.

Hospital CT scans usually have limited power, as live patients cannot tolerate high doses of radiation. In most cases they are powerful enough to look inside dinosaur fossils, but sometimes a high-powered industrial scanner is needed. Industrial scanners are also big, which comes in handy when examining a *T. rex*. (Tyrannosaurus Sue was put in a scanner normally used to view airplane parts!)

Paleontology may be the study of ancient things, but it is raising some new questions. Should developers be allowed to build a golf course over rare dinosaur trackways? Should dinosaur fossils be sold to private collectors who want to display them in their living rooms or turn them into coatracks? Should people be allowed to take dinosaur bones out of the country where they are found? Who will pay for museum displays, when excavating, preparing, and mounting a large skeleton can take ten years and easily cost a million dollars?

The Fiery End

Dinosaurs disappeared sixty-five million years ago. But they were already in decline in many areas of the world long before this, and there were fewer species. The climate was changing. Winters were colder and summers were warmer, and under these extreme conditions fewer kinds of plants and animals were able to survive. But many experts say that only an extraordinary event such as intense volcanic activity or an object from outer space could have finished off the dinosaurs so suddenly and dramatically.

In 1990 geologists found an ancient crater in Mexico. Rock samples date the crater to sixty-five million years ago, when an asteroid slammed into the earth. The explosion blasted chunks of rock so high that they left the atmosphere before falling back to Earth. Pieces the size of islands crashed down. Dust clouds blocked the sun, turning the world dark and cold. There were earthquakes and landslides, and huge tidal waves smashed into shorelines, flooding coastlines everywhere.

The collision was felt around the planet. As far away as New Zealand, ancient sediments have been found that were laid down at the same time the dinosaurs became extinct. These rocks contain high levels of iridium, a metal that is rare on Earth but common in meteors.

When the asteroid exploded, it is thought that flaming chunks of rock flew into forests, causing huge wildfires. Shock waves likely released pockets of gas from within the earth. The gas may have been ignited by lightning, setting the atmosphere itself on fire.

The Survivors

Not all life was wiped out sixty-five million years ago. Many species of small mammals, birds, turtles, crocodiles, lizards, and insects survived. They didn't need huge amounts of food, and could find refuge when disaster struck. Eventually several new species, including the ancestors of today's cats, wolves, and bears, began to flourish.

In the bleak years that followed, the heat trapped by the dust cloud may have caused global warming and acid rain, killing plants and marine life. Unable to cope with the sudden changes, more than half the species on the planet were wiped out, including the dinosaurs.

The dinosaur era ended with an asteroid. But it may have begun with one, too. In 2002 researchers reported evidence of another major asteroid impact that occurred 200 million years ago, just before dinosaurs became dominant.

Many large creatures were killed off, allowing the dog-sized dinos then in existence to eventually evolve into larger carnivores such as *T. rex*. The second impact may have killed off the dinosaurs but their descendants lived on. Some of them had already evolved into birds, which survived the extinction.

And that second asteroid did not wipe out evidence of the dinosaurs' existence, because every year we find more fossils. That means there are probably bigger, deadlier, and stranger dinosaurs still buried, just waiting to be found.

1. In 1997 in Alberta Canada, Phil Currie uncovered a pack of *Albertosaurus* dinos of different ages.

2. In 2001 in Montana, Jack Horner uncovered B. rex, an immature *T. rex* thought to be the oldest known *T. rex* to date.

3. Tyrannosaurus Sue was found in South Dakota in 1990.

4. The discovery of the first therizinosaur found in North America was announced in 2001. The turkey-sized *Nothronychus* was found in New Mexico near the Arizona border.

5. An asteroid estimated to have been 4 miles (6 km) in diameter crashed in the Yucatán peninsula 65 million years ago, ending the age of the dinosaurs.

6. In 2002 paleontologists reported finding in Argentina birdlike footprints 55 million years older than the oldest known bird fossils. Scientists are debating what kind of animal could have made the prints.

7. The announcement of what may be the oldest dinosaur ever found was made in 2001. The small, sharp-toothed creature was found in southern Brazil and could be an early stage in the evolution of dinosaurs.

8. *Giganotosaurus*, one of the biggest meat eaters ever, was discovered by Paul Sereno in Argentina in 1993.

9. The discovery of the large claw of *Megaraptor*, found in Patagonia in Argentina, was announced in 1998.

10. A huge titanosaur nesting ground, complete with fossilized eggs, was found in Patagonia in 1997 by Luis Chiappe, Lowell Dingus, and Rodolfo Coria.

11. *Eotyrannus*, a primitive tyrannosaur, was found on England's Isle of Wight in 1997.

12. In 2000 scientists announced the discovery of a new predator, *Saltriosaurus*, only the third dino species to be found in Italy.

13. The huge skull of *Carcharodontosaurus* was uncovered in the Sahara in 1995.

14. *Suchomimus* was found in 1997 in Niger, Africa.

15. *Jobaria* and *Nigersaurus*, two new sauropods, were discovered in Niger by Paul Sereno in 1997.

16. *Paralititan*, a massive titanosaur found in Egypt, was named in 2001.

17. Paleontologists reported the discovery of *Majungatholus* and *Masiakasaurus* in Madagascar in 1998.

18. In 2000 scientists announced the discovery in Mongolia of *Byronosaurus*. It had some features of modern-day birds including a large brain.

19. Northeast China continues to yield a treasure trove of dinosaur fossils. In 2002 Mark Norell announced the discovery of a theropod dinosaur with true feathers, closely linking it to modern birds.

20. The discovery in China of *Liaoceratops,* an ancient relative of *Triceratops*, was reported in 2002. The size of a poodle, the dino had the beginnings of horns and a frill.

21. *Qantassaurus*, a small plant eater named after Australia's airline, was found in 1999.

Glossary

aerodynamic: Used to describe a design or structure that reduces the drag of an object moving through air.

aorta: The main artery supplying blood from the heart to the rest of the body.

cardiologist: A doctor who studies the human heart.

carnivore: An animal that eats the flesh of another animal.

cartilage: Tough but flexible connective tissue attached to bones, usually near the joints.

colon: The lower part of the large intestine.

CT scan: A computerized image made from cross-sectional X rays of an object or person.

DNA: The abbreviation for deoxyribonucleic acid, a complex chemical compound found in cells that carries hereditary information.

electron microscope: A microscope that uses electron beams instead of light to create high magnification.

geologist: A scientist who studies the structure of the earth and the origin of rocks.

herbivore: An animal that eats only plant material.

mammal: A warm-blooded animal with fur or hair that nourishes its young with milk.

olfactory bulb: A rounded formation in the nasal cavity with sensitive nerves leading to the area of the brain responsible for the sense of smell.

raptor: A term once used only for birds of prey, it now also describes a group of smaller theropod dinosaurs with a large claw found on their second toe.

reptile: A cold-blooded animal usually covered with scales or horny plates.

sediment: Tiny pieces of soil or rock that are carried by water or wind and deposited on the surface of land or at the bottom of a lake.

species: A group of plants or animals with common characteristics.

tendon: A band of fibrous tissue connecting a muscle to a bone.

theropod: A large group of meat-eating dinosaurs that includes tyrannosaurs, therizinosaurs, and birds, among others.

ultraviolet light: Light with a wavelength shorter than the violet end of the visible spectrum. It allows scientists to see things not visible in ordinary light.

vertebrae: Plural form of "vertebra," one of the bony segments forming the spine.

vertebrate: An animal with vertebrae.

Pronunciation Guide

Achillobator:	**ah KILL oh BAH tore**
Albertosaurus:	**al BERT oh SORE us**
Allosaurus:	**AL oh SORE us**
Archaeopteryx:	**ark ee OP ter icks**
Argentinosaurus:	**AR jen TEE noh SORE us**
Bambiraptor:	**BAM bee RAP tor**
Byronosaurus:	**BYE ron oh SORE us**
Carcharodontosaurus:	**CAR CAR oh DON toe SORE us**
Carnotaurus:	**kar noh TORE us**
Diplodocus:	**dip PLOD oh kuss**
Eoraptor:	**EE oh RAP tore**
Eotyrannus:	**EE oh tye RAN us**
Giganotosaurus:	**JIG ah NOT oh SORE us**
Hypacrosaurus:	**hye PACK ro SORE us**
Jobaria:	**joe BAHR ee uh**
Liaoceratops:	**LYE oh SAIR ah tops**
Maiasaura:	**MY ah SORE ah**
Majungatholus:	**ma JUNG ah THOL us**
Masiakasaurus knopfleri:	**ma SHEE ah ka SORE us NOP flurrie**
Megaraptor:	**MEG ah RAP tore**
Microraptor:	**MY crow RAP tore**
Nanotyrannus:	**NAN oh tye RAN us**
Nigersaurus:	**nee ZHER SORE us**
Nothronychus:	**no throw NYE kuss**
Oviraptor:	**OH vih RAP tore**
Pachyrinosaurus:	**pack ih RINE oh SORE us**
Paralititan:	**pa RAL ih TYE tan**
Parasaurolophus:	**PAR ah sore AWL loff us**
pterosaur:	**TAIR oh sore**
Qantassaurus:	**KWAN tas SORE us**
Saltriosaurus:	**Salt REE oh SORE us**
Sarcosuchus imperator:	**SARK oh SOOK uss im pair AH tore**
Sauroposeidon:	**SORE oh poh SIDE on**
Scipionyx:	**SIP ee ON icks**
Seismosaurus:	**size mo SORE us**
Sinornithosaurus:	**sye NOR nith oh SORE us**
Styracosaurus:	**stye RACK oh SORE us**
Suchomimus:	**sue ko MY mus**
Tapejara imperator:	**tah pah HAR ah imp pair AH tore**
therizinosaur:	**THER ih ZEEN oh sore**
Thescelosaurus:	**THESS kel oh SORE us**
Triceratops:	**trye SAIR a tops**
Troodon:	**TROH oh don**
Tyrannosaurus rex:	**tye RAN oh SORE us rex**
Utahraptor:	**YOO tah RAP tore**
Velociraptor:	**vel OSS ih RAP tore**

Index

(Page numbers in italics refer to illustrations.)

A

Achillobator, 27
Africa, 16, 18, 45
Alberta, 10, 44
Albertosaurus, 14, *44*, 45
Allosaurus, 11
Antarctica, 18
Archaeopteryx, 24
Argentina, 18, 28, 34, 45
Argentinosaurus, 12, 14, 27, 28, 34
Arizona, 45
Asia, 18
asteroid, 41–43, *40*
Australia, 18, 45

B

Bambiraptor, *24–25*
bird, earliest, 24
bones, 2, 9, 10, 11, 19, 20, 28, 29, 34, 37, 39
Byronosaurus, 45, *45*

C

Canada, 14
Carcharodontosaurus, 4, 6, *44*, *45*
carnivores, 4, 12–13, 14, 16
Carnotaurus, 16, 18
Celeste, *T. rex*, 13
Chiappe, Luis, 45
China, 23, 27, 29, 34, 45
claws, 4, 19, 23, 26, *26–27*, 27
climate change, 41
clones, 38
cold-blooded, 21
coprolites, 32, 33, *32–33*
Coria, Rodolfo, 45
Cretaceous period, 18
crocodile, 6, 9, 14, 21, 27
CT scan, 3, 9, 20, 38, 39
Currie, Phil, 45

D

Dingus, Lowell, 45
dinosaurs
    and birds, 23, 24–25, 39, 43
    baby, 19, 34
    cannibals, 10
    care of young, 35
    descendants, 23, 43
    disappearance, 40–43
    discoveries, 2, 9, 18, 44–45
    families, 35, 36
    feathered, 23, 24, *24–25, 39*
    heaviest, 28
    longest, 28
    oldest, 18, *44*, 45
    smallest, 27
    sounds, 36, 37
    unnamed, 14, 28
Diplodocus, *28–29*
Dire Straits, 16
DNA, 3, 38
dung, 3, 32–33

E

eggs, 3, 34–35, *34, 35*
embryos, 34, *34*
England, 11, 45
Eoraptor, 18
Eotyrannus, 11, *44*, 45
Europe, Northern, 18

F

feathers, 3, 23, 24, 39
Field Museum, Chicago, 9
footprints, 29, *29*
fossils, 3, 9, 11,19, 23, 29, 32, 33, *36*, 38, 39, 41
frills, 21, 37, *37*

G

Giganotosaurus, 12, *12*, 13, *13*, 14, 27, *44*, 45
Gondwana, 18
Greenland, 18

H

head crests, 21, 36
hearing, 37
heart, 20, *20*, 21
Hendrikson, Sue, 9
Horner, Jack, 45
hunting, 14, 35
Hypacrosaurus, 14, *15*

I

India, 18
internal organs, 19, 20
Isle of Wight, 45
Italy, 19, 45

J

Jobaria, 5, *44*, 45
Jurassic Park, 19
Jurassic period, 18

K

Knopfler, Mark, 16

L

Laurasia, 18
Liaoceratops, *44*, 45
Liaoning, 23, 27
lizards, 21, 23

M

Madagascar, 16, 28, 45
Maiasaura, dung, 32
Majungatholus, 16, *16*, 18, *44*, 45
mammals, new species, 41
Masiakasaurus, 17, *17*, *44*, 45
    knopfleri, 16, *17*
Megaraptor, 26, 27, *44*, 45
Mexico, 41
Microraptor, 26, 27
Mongolia, 27, 45
Montana, 13, 35, 45
Morocco, 4

N

Nanotyrannus, 37
nesting grounds, 35, 45
New Mexico, 28, 36
New Zealand, 41
Niger, 4, 5, 6, 45
Nigersaurus, 5, *44*, 45
Norell, Mark, 45
North America, 11, 18
Nothronychus, *44*, 45

O

Oklahoma, 29
Oviraptor, 34, *35*

P

Pachyrhinosaurus, 37, *37*
paleontology, 39
Pangaea, 18
Paralititan, *44*, 45
Parasaurolophus, 36, *36*
Patagonia, 13, 14, 27, 28, 38, 45
prey, 4, 9, 12, 14, 21, 37
pterosaurs, 24–25

Q

Qantassaurus, *44*, 45

R

raptors, 14, 26–27
reptiles, 6, 21, 39
    flying, 24–25, *24–25*

S

Sahara, 4, 38, 45
Saltriosaurus, *44*, 45
Sarcosuchus imperator, 6
sauropods, *3*, 4, 5, *5*, 6, 7, 14, 28–29, *28–29*, 30, *30–31*, *32–33*, 34
    eating habits, 30
    footprints, 29, *29*
    tails, 29
Sauroposeidon, 29
Scipionyx, 19, *19*
Seismosaurus, 28
Sereno, Paul, 45
Sinornithosaurus, 22, 23
skeleton, 6, 9, 13, 19, *24–25*, 34, 35, 39
skin, 19, 34, 37
South America, 16, 18, 27
South Dakota, 9, 13, 20, 45

Steven, *T. rex*, 10
Styracosaurus, *1*, 37, *37*
Suchomimus, 4, 6, 14, *44*, 45
Sue, 9, 10–11, *12*, 39, *44*, 45
SuperCroc, 6, *6–7*

T

T. rex, 4, 8–11, *8–9*, *10–11*, 13, *13*, 14, 39, *44*, 45
    biggest, 13
    bite force, 9
    brain, 8, 9
    eating habits, 10, 32
    sense of smell, 9
    walking, 10–11, *10–11*
tails, 10, 14, 29
Tapejara imperator, 25, *24–25*
teeth, 4, 5, 6, 12, 13, 17, 19, 23, 34
therizinosaur, 34, *34*, 45
theropods, 19, 23, 45
Thescelosaurus, 20, *20–21*
titanosaurs, 33, 34, 45
Triassic period, 18
Triceratops, 45
Troodon, 35
tyrannosaurs, 10, 14, *15*, 45
Tyrannosaurus rex, 2, 13 (see also *T. rex*)
Tyrannosaurus Sue, (see Sue)

U

Utahraptor, 14, *14*

V

Velociraptor, 2, 11, 14, 23, 27, *38–39*, 39

W

warm-blooded, 21
Willo, 20, *20–21*

Y

Yucatán peninsula, 45

Web Sites

www.bbc.co.uk/dinosaurs/
Site of BBC television's acclaimed series, Walking with Dinosaurs.

www.fmnh.org/sue/
Chicago's Field Museum of Natural History offers all sorts of fascinating information on *Tyrannosaurus* Sue.

www.projectexploration.org/jobaria/index.html
http://dinosaur.uchicago.edu/Suchomimus.html
www.supercroc.com
These three sites look at the latest details on *Jobaria*, *Suchomimus,* and SuperCroc. All were created by Project Exploration, a nonprofit educational organization founded by Paul Sereno and Gabrielle Lyon.

www.tyrrellmuseum.com
Site of one of the world's foremost paleontology institutions, the Royal Tyrrell Museum.

Recommended Reading

Feathered Dinosaurs
by Christopher Sloan, National Geographic
An exciting look at the links between dinosaurs and birds.

The Kingfisher Illustrated Dinosaur Encyclopedia
by David Burnie, illustrated by John Sibbick
An informative reference book filled with remarkable illustrations.

Picture Credits

All illustrations are by Alan Barnard unless otherwise stated.

p. 10:   *(Bottom)* IH034131
© CORBIS/MAGMA
p. 18:   *(Bottom)* Maps by Jack McMaster
p. 19:   *(Top)* Courtesy Museo Civico di Storia Naturale, Milano (Italy). Photo by F. Valoti, artwork by F. Fogliazza.
(Bottom) Soprintendenza per i Beni Archeologici, Salerno (Italy)

p. 20:   *(Right)* J. Page, North Carolina Museum of Natural Sciences
p. 29:   *(Top, right)* 0000378060-024 © Vo Trung Dung/CORBIS SYGMA/MAGMA
pp. 32–33: *(Bottom)* © The Natural History Museum, London.
p. 36:   *(Top)* AF004548 © Kevin Schafer/CORBIS/MAGMA. *(Bottom)* FT0083075 © AFP/CORBIS/MAGMA
pp. 44–45: Maps and diagrams by Jack McMaster

Acknowledgments

I would like to thank my parents for starting me on this path by introducing me to the works of Rudolph Zallinger, Jay Matternes, and Ray Harryhausen. This book is for my wife, Michelle, and for our daughters, Rebecca and Katherine, who never complained about me spending so much time in the Mesozoic. — *Alan Barnard*

Shelley Tanaka and Madison Press Books would like to extend their thanks to Philip Currie, Kevin Seymour, Marco Signore, Peter Brand, and Brenda Bowen, Caitlyn Dlouhy, Susan Burke, Jeannie Ng and the editors at Atheneum Books for Young Readers.

Illustrations copyright © 2002 Alan Barnard. Text, jacket, design, and compilation copyright © 2002 The Madison Press Limited.

Library of Congress
Cataloging-in-Publication Data

Tanaka, Shelley.
New dinos : The latest finds! The coolest dinosaur discoveries! / Shelley Tanaka ; illustrated by Alan Barnard.
      p. cm.
Summary: Describes some of the newly discovered dinosaurs and what paleontologists have learned about these prehistoric creatures in recent years.

ISBN 0-689-85183-9
1. Dinosaurs—Juvenile literature.
[1. Dinosaurs. 2. Paleontology.]
I. Barnard, Alan, ill.   II. Title.
QE861.5.T36 2003
567.9—dc21   2002009809

10 9 8 7 6 5 4 3 2 1

Editorial Director: Hugh Brewster
Art Director: Gord Sibley
Graphic Production: Nathan Beyerle
Project Editors: Susan Aihoshi, Mireille Majoor
Editorial Assistance: Nan Froman, Imoinda Romain
Production Director: Susan Barrable
Production Manager: Sandra L. Hall
Color Separation: Colour Technologies
Printing and Binding: Imago Productions (F.E.) Ltd., Singapore

New Dinos was produced by Madison Press Books, which is under the direction of Albert E. Cummings.

Madison Press Books
1000 Yonge Street, Suite 200
Toronto, Ontario
Canada M4W 2K2

Printed in Singapore